Daydreaming for Inspiration

Published by
Your Business Matters Limited

7 Swan Court, Forder Way,
Hampton, Peterborough,
Cambridgeshire PE7 8GX
United Kingdom

ISBN 978-0-9556563-0-9

Daydreaming for Inspiration

Compiled by Stephen Pauley
and Judith Underhill

Design and Illustration
by Emma Proctor

Published by
Your Business Matters Limited
United Kingdom

always

create your own

dreams

and
live
life
to the

fullest

By Susan Polis Schutz

1

{Dreams} **can** come true If you take the
time to think about what you want in life
Get to know yourself
find out who **you** are
Choose your goals carefully
Be honest with yourself
Always **believe** in yourself
Find many interests and pursue them
Find out what is **IMPORTANT** to you
Find out what you are good at
Don't be afraid to make mistakes
Work hard to achieve successes
When things are not going right
don't give up – just try harder!
Give yourself freedom to
try out new things
Laugh and have a good time
Open yourself up to (love)
Take part in the beauty of nature
Be appreciative of all that you have
Help those less fortunate than you
Work towards peace in the world
(Live life to the fullest)
Create your own dreams and follow
them until they are a reality

People are often unreasonable,
Illogical, and self-centered;
Forgive them anyway.

If you are kind,
People may accuse you of selfish, ulterior motives;
Be kind anyway.

If you are successful,
You will win some false friends and some true enemies;
Succeed anyway.

If you are honest and frank,
People may cheat you;
Be honest and frank anyway.

What you spend years building,
Someone could destroy overnight;
Build anyway.

If you find serenity and happiness,
They may be jealous;
Be happy anyway.

The good you do today,
People will often forget tomorrow;
Do good anyway.

Give the world the best you have,
And it may never be enough;
Give the world the best you've got anyway.

You see, in the final analysis,
It is between you and God;
It never was between you and them anyway.
Be Blessed,

Mother Teresa

If I Knew

If I knew it would be the last time that I'd see
you fall asleep I would tuck you up more tightly.
If I knew it would be the last time that I see you
walk out the door I would give you a hug and a kiss
and call you back for one more.
If I knew it would be the last time I'd hear your
voice lifted up in praise I would video tape each
action and word so I could play them back day
after day.
If I knew it would be the last time I could spare
an extra minute to stop and say "I Love You" instead
of assuming you would know I do.
If I knew it would be the last time I would be there
to share your day, Well I'm sure you'll have so many
more so I can let this one just slip away. For surely
there's always tomorrow to make up for an oversight
and we always get a second chance to make everything just right.
There always be another day to say "I Love You"
and certainly there's another chance to say our
"anything I can do?"
But just in case I might be wrong and today is all
I get I'd like to say how much I love you and I
hope we never forget.
Tomorrow is not promised to anyone, young or old alike.
And today may be the last chance you get to hold
your love ones tight

So if you're waiting for tomorrow, why not do it today?
For if tomorrow never comes you'll surely regret the day
That you didn't take that extra time for a smile, a
hug, or a kiss and you were too busy to grant someone,
what turned out to be their one last wish.
So hold your loved ones close today and whisper in
their ear.
Tell them how much you love them and you'll always
hold them dear take time to say "I'm sorry", "please
forgive me", "thank you", or "it's okay".
And if tomorrow never comes you'll have no regrets
about today.

Norma Cornett Marek

Our deepest fear is not that we are inadequate. Our deepest fear is that we are **powerful** beyond measure.

It is our light not our **darkness** that most frightens us. We ask ourselves, "who am I to be brilliant, *gorgeous,* talented, fabulous?"

Actually, who are you not to be?

you are a child of God. your playing small does not serve the world, there is nothing enlightening about shrinking so that other people won't feel insecure around us.

We are meant to shine, as children do. We are born to manifest the glory of God that is within us.

It is not just in some of us - it is in **EVERYONE** and as we let our light shine we unconsciously give other people permission to do the same.

As we are liberated from our fear our presence automatically liberates others.

Nelson Mandella
(used in his inaugural speech but taken from Return To Love By Marianne Williamson).

shine

We are meant to shine, as children do

If I had my life to live over,

I'd dare to make more mistakes next time.

I'd relax. I'd limber up.

I would be sillier than I have this time.

I would take fewer things seriously.

I would take **more** chances.

I would take **more** trips *Timbuktu*

I would climb more mountains

And swim more rivers

I could eat **more** ice cream and less beans.

I would perhaps have **more** actual troubles

But I'd have fewer imaginary ones.

You see, I am one of those people

9

Who live sensibly and sanely

Hour after hour, day after day.

Oh, I've had my <u>moments</u>

And if I had to do it all over again,
I'd have **more** of them.

In fact I'd try to do nothing else.

Just moments, one after the other,

Instead of living so many years

ahead of each day.

If I had my life to live over,

I would start barefoot early in the spring

And I would stay that way until late into the Autumn.

I would go to **more** dances,

I would ride more merry-go-rounds

I would pick more daisies.

Nadine Stair

Bad times, hard times —
this is what people keep saying;
But let us live well,
and times shall be good.
We are the times:
Such as we are,
such are the times.

St. Augustine

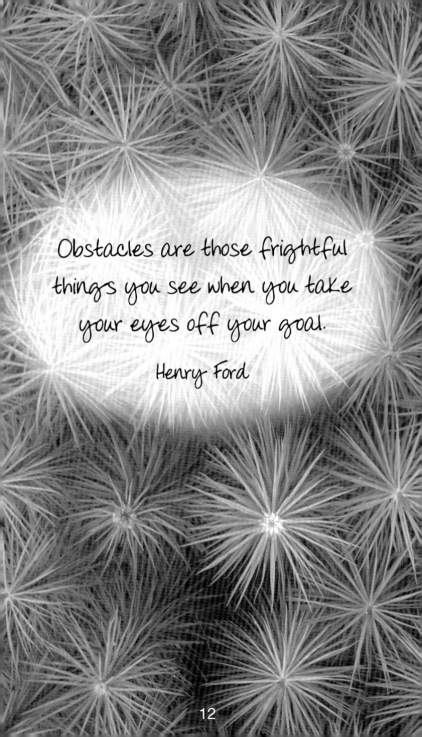

Obstacles are those frightful things you see when you take your eyes off your goal.

Henry Ford

From ' By The River Of Piedra
I Sat Down And Wept'

Every day, God gives us the sun – and also one moment in which we have the ability to change everything that makes us unhappy. Every day, we try to pretend that we haven't perceived that moment, that it doesn't exist – that today is the same as yesterday and will be the same as tomorrow. But if people really pay attention to their every day lives, they will discover that magic moment. It may arrive in the instant when we are doing something mundane, like putting our front door key in the lock; it may lie hidden in the quiet that follows the lunch hour or in the thousand and one things that all seem the same to us. But that moment exists – a moment when the power of all the stars become part of us and enables us to perform miracles.

Joy is sometimes a blessing, but is often a conquest. Our magic moment helps us to change and sends us off in search of our dreams. Yes, we are going to suffer, we will have difficult times, and we will experience many disappointments – but all of this is transitory; it leaves no permanent mark. And one day we will look back with pride and faith at the journey we have taken.

Pitiful is the person who is afraid to take risks.
Perhaps this person will never be disappointed or
disillusioned; perhaps they won't suffer the way
people do when they have a dream to follow. But
when that person looks back – and at sometime
everyone looks back – they will hear their heart
saying "What have you done with the miracles that
God planted in your days? What have you done
with the talents God bestowed on you? You buried
yourself in a cave because you were fearful of
losing those talents. So this is your heritage: the
certainty that you wasted your life."

Pitiful are the people that realise this. Because
when they are finally able to believe in miracles,
their life's magic moments will have passed them by.

Paulo Coelho

Be Glad Of Life

Because it gives you the chance to love and
to work and to play and to look up at the
stars; to be satisfied with your possessions;
to despise nothing in the world except
falsehood and meanness, to fear nothing
except cowardice; to be governed by your
admirations rather than by your disgusts; to
covet nothing that is your neighbour's
except his kindness of heart and gentleness
of manners; to think seldom of your enemies,
often of your friends....and to spend as much
time as you can, with body and with spirit.

These are little guideposts on the
footpath to peace.

Henry van Dyke

BELIEVE IN YOURSELF
(and remember) that ANYTHING is possible !!

Believe in what makes you feel good and what makes you happy.

Believe in all the dreams you've always wanted to come true, and give them every chance to.

If you are willing to take the opportunities you are given and utilize the abilities you have, you will constantly fill your life with special moments and unforgettable times.

No one knows the mysteries of life or it's ultimate meaning, but for those who are willing to believe in their dreams and in themselves life is a precious gift in which anything is possible.

Dena Dilaconi

16

May today there be peace within.

May you trust your highest power that you are exactly where you are meant to be.

May you not forget the infinite possibilities that are born of faith.

May you use those gifts that you have received, and pass on the love that has been given to you.

May you be content knowing you are a child of God.

Let this presence settle into our bones, and allow your soul the freedom to sing, dance, praise and love.

It is there for each and every one of you!

The Serenity Prayer

God, grant me the serenity
to accept the things
I cannot change;
the courage to change
the things I can;
and the wisdom to know
the difference.

Reinhold Neibuhr

We are all travellers on a cosmic journey – stardust, swirling and dancing in the eddies and whirlpools of infinity.
Life is eternal.

But the expressions of life are ephemeral, momentary, transient. This existence of ours is as transient as autumn clouds.

To watch the birth and death of beings is like looking at the movements of dance.

A life time is like a flash of lightning across the sky – rushing by like a torrent down a steep mountain.

We have stopped for a moment to encounter each other, to meet, to love, to share. This is a precious moment but it is transient. It is a little parenthesis in eternity.

If we share with caring, light heartedness, and love, we create abundance and joy for each other - and then this moment has been worthwhile.

Deepak Chopra

Heaven's Grocery Store

As I was walking down life's highway, many years ago,
I came upon a sign that read, Heaven's Grocery Store.

When I got a little closer, the doors swung open wide
And when I came to myself, I was standing inside.
I saw a host of angels, they were standing everywhere.
One handed me a basket, and said "my child shop
with care".

Everything a human needed, was in that grocery store.
And what you could not carry, you could come back
for more. First I got some patience, love was in that
same row. Further down was understanding, you need
that everywhere you go.

I got a box or two of wisdom, and faith a bag or two.
And charity of course, I would need some of that too.
I couldn't miss the Holy Ghost, it was all over the place.
And then some strength and courage to help me run
this race.

My basket was getting full but I remembered I needed
grace and then I chose salvation, for salvation was free
– I tried to get enough of that to do for you and me.

Then I started to the counter to pay my grocery bill
For I thought I had everything to do the Masters will.
As I went up the aisle, I saw prayer and put that in for I
knew when I stepped outside I would run right into sin.

Peace and joy were plentiful, the last things on the shelf, song and praise were hanging near, so I just helped myself. Then I said to the Angel "Now how much do I owe?" He just smiled and said "Just take them everywhere you go".

Again I asked "Really now, How much do I owe?" "My child" he said "God paid your bill a long, long time ago".

Ron De Marco

Start by doing
what is necessary,
then do what's
possible, and
suddenly you
are doing the
impossible.

St Francis of Assisi

You Change the World

Ten thoughts to help you avoid discouragement

1. Look at life as a journey and enjoy the ride. Get the most out of detours and realise they are sometimes necessary.

2. Do your best, but if what you have been doing has caused you discouragement, try a different approach. Be passionate about the process, but don't be so attached to the outcome.

3. Wish the best for everyone, with no personal strings attached. Applaud someone else's win as much as you would your own.

4. Trust that we will not always know what is best for us. A disappointment now could mean a victory later, so don't be disappointed. There is usually a reason.

5. Ask no more of yourself than the very best you can do. Be compassionate towards yourself as well as others. Know your calling, your gift and do it well.

6. Don't worry about something after it's done; it's out of your hands then, too late, over! Learn the lesson and move on.

7. Have the attitude that no one, except you, owes you anything. Give without expecting a thank you in return. But when someone does something for you, be appreciative of even the smallest gestures.

8. Choose your thoughts or your thoughts will choose you; they will free you or keep you bound. Educate your spirit and give it authority over your feelings.

9. Judge no one, and disappointment and forgiveness won't be an issue. No one can let you down if you're not leaning on them. People can't hurt you unless you allow them to.

10. Love anyway… for no reason… and give… just because.

Donna Fargo

A Beautiful Prayer

I asked God to take away my habit
God said No
It is not for me to take away,
but for you to give up.

I asked God to make
handicapped children whole
God said No
Their spirits are whole,
their bodies only temporary.

I asked God to grant me patience
God said No
Patience is a by product of tribulations;
It isn't granted it is learned.

I asked God to give me happiness
God said No
I give you blessings;
Happiness is up to you.

I asked God to spare me pain
God said No
Suffering draws you apart from worldly cares
And brings you closer to me.

I asked God to make my spirit grow
God said No
You must grow on your own
But I will prune you to
make you more fruitful.

I asked God for all the things
I might enjoy in life
God said No
I shall give you life
So that you may enjoy all things.

I asked God to help me love others
As much as he loves me
God said ahhhh, finally you have the idea.

To the world you might be one person
But to one person you might just be the world.

Miss Joanne Gobure from Uaboe in Nauru

I Will Not Die An Unlived Life

I will not die an unlived life.
I will not live in fear
of falling or catching fire.
I choose to inhabit my days,
to allow my living to open me,
to make me less afraid,
more accessible;
to loosen my heart
until it becomes a wing,
a torch, a promise.
I choose to risk my significance,
to live so that which came to me as
seed goes to the next as blossom,
and that which came to me as
blossom, goes on as fruit.

Dawna Markova

Listen to the Mustn'ts, child,
Listen to the Don'ts,
Listen to the Shouldn'ts,
The Impossibles,
The Won'ts,
Listen to the Never Haves;
Then listen close to me—
Anything can happen, child,
Anything can be

"Listen, Child"
Shel Silverstein
(Children's Book Writer)

31

Go confidently in the
direction of your dreams!
Live the life you've imagined.

Thoreau

Set Yourself Free

Set yourself free from anything that might hinder you in becoming the person you want to be. Free yourself from the uncertainties about your abilities or the worth of your dreams, from the fears that you may not be able to achieve them or that they won't be what you wanted.

Set yourself free from the past. The good things from yesterday are still yours in memory; the things you want to forget you will, for tomorrow is only a sunrise away. Free yourself from regret or guilt, and promise to live this day as fully as you can.

Set yourself free from the expectations of others, and never feel guilty or embarrassed if you do not live up to their standards. You are most important to yourself; live by what you feel is best and right for you. Others will come to respect your integrity and honesty.

Set yourself free to simply be yourself, and you will soar higher than you've ever dreamed.

Edmund O'Neill

The Essense of Achievement

"The *credit* belongs to those people who are actually in the arena…who know the great *enthusiasms*, the great devotions to a worthy cause; who at best, know the TRIUMPH of high achievement; and who, at worst, fail while daring GREATLY, so that their place shall never be with those cold and timid souls who know neither **VICTORY** nor defeat."

Theodore Roosevelt

Do not retreat into your private world,
That place of safety, sheltered from the storm
Where you may tend your garden, seek your soul,
And rest with loved ones where the fire burns warm.

To tend a garden is a precious thing,
But dearer still the one where all may roam,
The weeds of poison, poverty and war,
Demand your care, who call the earth your home.

To seek your soul it is a precious thing,
But you will never find it on your own,
Only among the clamour, threat and pain
Of other people's need will love be known.

To rest with loved ones is a precious thing,
But peace of mind exacts a higher cost,
Your children will not rest and play in quiet,
While they hear the crying of the lost.

Do not retreat into your private world,
There are more ways than firesides to keep warm;
There is not shelter from the ranges of life
So meet its eye, and dance within the storm.

Kathy Galloway

As we grow up, we learn that even the one person that wasn't supposed to ever let you down probably will.

You will have your heart broken probably more than once and it's harder every time.

You'll break hearts too, so remember how it felt when yours was broken.

You'll fight with your best friend.

You'll blame a new love for things an old one did.

You'll cry because time is passing too fast, and you'll eventually lose someone you love.

So take too many pictures, laugh too much, and love like you've never been hurt, because, every sixty seconds you spend upset is a minute of happiness you'll **NEVER** get back

Chat, chat, natter

TISSUES

Cheese!

I ♥ U

POT OF GOLD

40

Never doubt
that a small group of
thoughtful, committed citizens
can change the world. Indeed it
is the only thing that ever
has. Margaret Mead

DON'T QUIT

When things go wrong, as they sometimes will,
when the road you're trudging seems all uphill,
when the funds are low and the debts are high,
and you want to smile but you have to sigh,
when care is pressing you down a bit - rest if
you must, but don't you quit.

Life is queer with its twists and turns.
As everyone of us sometimes learns.
And many a fellow turns about when he might
have won had he stuck it out.

Don't give up though the pace seems slow -
you may succeed with another blow.
Often the goal is nearer than it seems to a faint
and faltering man; often the struggler has
given up when he might have captured the
victor's cup; and he learned too late when the
night came down, how close he was to the
golden crown.

Success is failure turned inside out - the silver
tint of the clouds of doubt, and when you
never can tell how close you are,
it may be near when it seems afar; so stick to
the fight when you're hardest hit - it's when
things seem worst, you must not quit

Edgar A. Guest

Oh, I have
slipped
the

surly bonds of earth and
danced the skies on laughter-silvered
wings; sunward I've climbed and joined the
tumbling mirth of sun-split clouds - and done a
hundred things you have not dreamed of; wheeled
and soared and swung high in the sun-lit silence.
Hovering there I've chased the shouting wind along,
and flung my eager craft through footless halls of air;
up, up the long, delirious, burning blue I've topped the
wind-swept heights with easy grace, where never
lark nor even eagle flies; and while, with silent
lifting mind I've trod the high untrespassed
sanctity of space, put out my hand,
and touched the face of God.

John Gillespie Magee

Twelve Things To Remember
(And One Thing Never To Forget)

1. Your presence is a present to the world.
2. You're unique and one of a kind.
3. Your life can be what you want it to be.
4. Take the days just one at a time.
5. Count your blessings not your troubles.
6. You'll make it through whatever comes along.
7. Within you are so many answers.
8. Understand, have courage, be strong.
9. Realize that it's never too late.
10. Do ordinary things in an extraordinary way.
11. Have health and hope and happiness.
12. Take the time to wish upon a star.

And don't ever forget for even a day
how very special you are.

Colin McCartney

ON LISTENING

WHEN I ASK YOU TO LISTEN TO ME AND YOU START BY GIVING ME ADVICE YOU HAVE NOT DONE WHAT I HAVE ASKED.

WHEN I ASK YOU TO LISTEN TO ME AND YOU BEGIN BY TELLING ME WHY I SHOULDN'T FEEL THAT WAY. YOU ARE TRAMPLING ON MY FEELINGS.

WHEN I ASK YOU TO LISTEN TO ME AND YOU FEEL YOU HAVE TO SOLVE MY PROBLEMS. YOU HAVE FAILED ME. STRANGE AS IT MAY SEEM.

LISTEN!

ALL I ASK IS THAT YOU LISTEN. NOT TALK OR DO .. JUST HEAR ME. WHEN YOU DO SOMETHING FOR ME THAT I CAN DO FOR MYSELF. YOU CONTRIBUTE TO MY FEAR AND INADEQUACY.

AND I CAN DO FOR MYSELF. I'M NOT HELPLESS.

MAYBE DISCOURAGED AND FALTERING. BUT NOT HELPLESS.

BUT. WHEN YOU ACCEPT AS SIMPLE FACT THAT I DO FEEL WHAT I FEEL. NO MATTER HOW IRRATIONAL. THEN I CAN QUIT TRYING TO CONVINCE YOU AND GET ABOUT THE BUSINESS OF UNDERSTANDING WHAT'S BEHIND THIS IRRATIONAL FEELING.

AND WHEN THAT'S CLEAR THE ANSWERS ARE
OBVIOUS – AND I DON'T NEED ADVICE.

IRRATIONAL FEELINGS MAKE SENSE WHEN WE
UNDERSTAND WHAT IS BEHIND THEM.

PERHAPS THAT'S WHY PRAYER WORKS. SOMETIMES.
FOR SOME PEOPLE.
BECAUSE GOD IS MUTE. AND DOESN'T GIVE ADVICE
OR TRY TO FIX THINGS.

GOD JUST LISTENS AND LETS YOU WORK IT OUT FOR
YOURSELF.

SO. PLEASE LISTEN AND JUST HEAR ME. AND IF YOU
WANT TO TALK WAIT A MINUTE FOR YOUR TURN AND I
WILL GLADLY LISTEN TO YOU.

RALPH ROUGHTON

Aim Higher

Always aim higher than you believe
you can reach. So often, you'll
discover that when your talents
are set free by your imagination,
you can achieve any goal.

If people offer their help or wisdom
as you go through life, accept it
gratefully. You can learn much from
those who have gone before you.

But never be afraid or hesitant to
step off the accepted path and
head off in your own direction,
if your heart tells you that it's
the right way for you.

Always believe that you will ultimately succeed at whatever you do, and never forget the value of persistence, discipline, and determination.

YOU ARE MEANT TO BE WHATEVER YOU DREAM OF BECOMING

By Edmund O'Neill

48

WHEN I WAS YOUNG AND
FREE AND MY IMAGINATION
HAD NO LIMITS, I DREAMED I
COULD CHANGE THE WORLD.
AS I GREW OLDER AND WISER,
I REALISED THE WORLD
WOULD NOT CHANGE. AND I
DECIDED TO SHORTEN MY
SIGHTS SOMEWHAT AND
CHANGE ONLY MY COUNTRY.
BUT IT SEEMED IMMOVABLE.

AS I ENTERED MY TWILIGHT
YEARS, IN ONE LAST
DESPERATE ATTEMPT, I
SOUGHT TO CHANGE ONLY
MY FAMILY, THOSE CLOSEST
TO ME; BUT ALAS THEY
WOULD HAVE NONE OF IT.

AND NOW HERE I LIE IN MY
DEATH BED AND REALISE,
PERHAPS FOR THE FIRST
TIME, THAT IF ONLY I HAD
CHANGED MYSELF FIRST,
THEN BY EXAMPLE I MAY
HAVE INFLUENCED MY
FAMILY AND WITH THEIR
ENCOURAGEMENT AND
SUPPORT I MAY HAVE
BETTERED MY COUNTRY,
AND WHO KNOWS, I MAY
HAVE CHANGED THE WORLD

FROM A BISHOP'S TOMB,
WESTMINSTER ABBEY CIRCA 1100AD

CHANGE

Success

To laugh often and much,

To win the respect of
intelligent people and the
affection of children,

To earn the appreciation of
honest critics and endure the
betrayal of false friends,

To appreciate the beauty,

To find the best in others!

To leave the world a bit
better, whether by a
healthy child, a garden
patch or a redeemed
social condition,

To know even one life
has breathed easier
because you have lived.

This is to have succeeded.

Ralph Waldo Emerson

The Road Not Taken

Two roads diverged in a yellow wood,
And sorry I could not travel both
And be one traveller, long I stood
And looked down one as far as I could
To where it bent in the undergrowth;

Then took the other, as just as fair,
And having perhaps the better claim,
Because it was grassy and wanted wear;
Though as for that the passing there
Had worn them really about the same,

And both that morning equally lay
In leaves no step had trodden black.
Oh, I kept the first for another day!
Yet knowing how way leads on to way,
I doubted if I should ever come back.

I shall be telling this with a sigh
Somewhere ages and ages hence:
Two roads diverged in a wood,
And I took the one less travelled by,
And that has made all the difference

Robert Frost

Five Balls,
From the Book
"Suzanne's Diary to Nicholas"

Imagine life as a game in which you are
juggling some five balls in the air.
You name them – Work – Family – Health –
Friends – Spirit, and you're keeping all of
these in the air.
You will soon understand that work is a
rubber ball. If you drop it, it will bounce back.
But the other four balls -- family, health,
friends and spirit are made of glass. If you
drop one of these, they will be irrevocably
scuffed, marked, nicked, damaged or even
shattered.
They will never be the same. You must
understand that and strive for balance
in your life. How?

1. Don't undermine your worth by comparing
yourself with others. It is because we are
different that each of us is special.

2. Don't set your goals by what other people
deem important. Only you know what is best
for you

3. Don't take for granted the things closest
to your heart. Cling to them as you would
your life, for without them, life is meaningless.

4. Don't let your life slip through your fingers by living in the past or for the future. By living your life one day at a time, you live ALL the days of your life.

5. Don't give up when you still have something to give. Nothing is really over until the moment you stop trying.

6. Don't be afraid to admit that you are less than perfect. It is this fragile thread that binds us together.

7. Don't be afraid to encounter risks. It is by taking chances that we learn how to be brave.

8. Don't shut love out of your life by saying it's impossible to find. The quickest way to receive love is to give; the fastest way to lose love is to hold it too tightly; and the best way to keep love is to give it wings.

9. Don't run through life so fast that you forget not only where you've been, but also where you are going.

10. Don't forget that a person's greatest emotional need is to feel appreciated.

11. Don't be afraid to learn. Knowledge is weightless, a treasure you can always carry easily.

12. Don't use time or words carelessly. Neither can be retrieved.

James Patterson

We do not believe in ourselves until someone reveals that deep inside us something is valuable, worth listening to, worthy of our trust, sacred to our touch. Once we believe in ourselves we can risk curiosity, wonder, spontaneous delight or any experience that reveals the human spirit.

EE Cummings

55

You are here to enable the world to live
more amply, with greater vision and with
a finer spirit of hope and achievement.
You are here to enrich the world.

Woodrow Wilson.

"Twenty years from now you will be more disappointed by the things you didn't do than by the ones you did. So throw off the bowlines. Sail away from the safe harbour. Catch the trade winds in your sails. Explore. Dream. Discover."?

Mark Twain

Explore.
Dream.
Discover

Too often we underestimate the power of a touch, a smile, a kind word, a listening ear, an honest compliment or the smallest act of caring, all of which have the potential to turn a life around.

Leo Buscaglia

hello there!

you're _so_ good at that

IS THAT A NEW TOP?

I wonder if she'd like to talk about it?

THANKS

you've got a lovely smile!

cup of tea?

Are you ok?

I couldn't have done it _without you!_

Can I help you with that?

Love you ✕

come round for dinner one night...

LET ME GIVE YOU A HUG

have you had your hair done

"First, when everybody tells you that you are being idealistic or impractical, consider the possibility that everybody could be wrong about what is right for you.

Look inside yourself the way nobody else can.

Will the pursuit of your dream hurt anybody?

Do you stand at least a fair chance of success?

If you fail, will you be seriously damaged or merely embarrassed?

If you succeed, will it change your life for the better?

When you can persuade yourself that your dream is worthwhile and achievable--then you say thank you to the doubters and take the plunge

...How much better to know that we have dared to live our dreams than to live our lives in a lethargy of regret."

Gilbert E. Kaplan

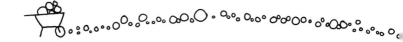

61

Instructions

When I have moved beyond you in the
adventure of life,
Gather in some pleasant place and
there remember me
With spoken words, old and new.
Let a tear or two if you will, but let
a smile come quickly
For I have loved the laughter of life.
Do not linger too long with your solemnities.

Go eat and talk, and when you can;
Follow a woodland trail, climb a
high mountain,
Sleep beneath the stars, swim a cold river,
Chew the thoughts of some book
Which challenges your soul.

Use your hands some bright day
To make a thing of beauty
Or to lift someone's heavy load.
Though you mention not my name,
Though no thought of me crosses your mind,
I shall be with you,
For these have been the realities of
life for me.

.And when you face some crisis
with anguish.
When you walk alone with courage,
When you choose your path of right,
When you give yourself in love,
I shall be very close to you.
I have followed the valleys,
I have climbed the heights of life.

Arnold Compton

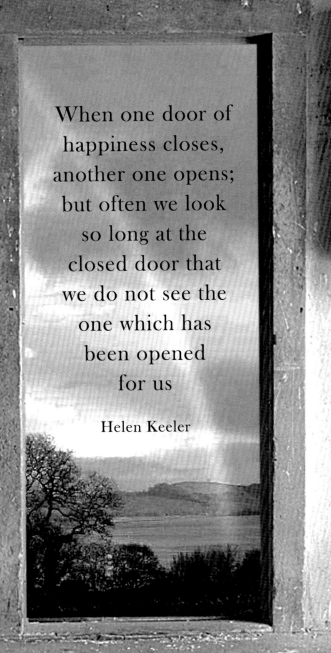

When one door of
happiness closes,
another one opens;
but often we look
so long at the
closed door that
we do not see the
one which has
been opened
for us

Helen Keeler

For additional information on the services and products offered by Your Business Matters Limited please visit our website at www.your-business-matters.com